BUCK NELSON'S TRIP TO MARS, MOON & VENUS: THE FBI FILE Historical Documents For the Study of The Modern UFO Era

Carlos Allende

SAUCERIAN PUBLISHER

ISBN:978-1-955087-13-1

© 2022,Saucerian Publisher

All rights reserved. No part of this publication maybe reproduced, translate, store in a retrieval system, or transmitted in any form or by any means, electronic, mechanical, photocopying, recording or otherwise, without prior written permision from the publisher.

Buck Nelson (1894-1982) holding up a sign for one of his spacecraft conventions with the "S" written backwards.

Buck Nelson

Bob Palmer sits at the registration desk at Buck Nelson's Spacecraft Convention ready to sell visitors copies of *My Trip to Mars, the Moon and Venus* by Mr. Nelson.

James L. Hill of Seymour, Missouri.

Prologue

Over the years, there have been rumors suggesting that various agencies of the US Government have extensive background files on the contactees. The FBI opened files on numerous well-known figures in the UFO contactee field. However, where are the less prominent figures of this era like Michael X Barton, Gloria Lee, Partana Vegan and many other?. As a result of our mission to publish books on Flying Saucers, Paranormal, Hermetica & the Occult Science, we have tried to obtain the FBI's files on such contactees as Frank Stranges, George Van Tassel, Truman Bethurum, George Adamski, George Hunt Williamson, Michael X, Gloria Lee, Orfeo Angelucci and Buck Nelson.

Carl Jung became fascinated or even obsessed with one of the most picturesque and interesting contactees of the UFO era. Jung put Orfeo Angelucci in his last book: *Flying Saucers: A Modern Myth of Things Seen in the Sky* (1959). Even he said that Orfeo had made up a "new bible." It is possible that if it hadn't been for Carl Jung, most people would never have read Orfeo Angelucci's. But Orfeo's FBI file was destroyed by the FBI years back. However, another contactee has almost completed his FBI File, which seems to be Angelucci's twin soul; he is Buck Nelson. Nelson was one of the most unusual of the mid-1950s so-called contactees. We don't know why Jung missed Buck.

Buck Nelson's completed FBI file has around 62 pages, including his book entitled: *My trip to Mars, the Moon, and Venus*. It seems Hoover's Men in Black took the writings of this Ozark Mountain farmer seriously. Nelson's story was transcribed by a compatriot, Fanny Lowery.

Buck Nelson was the subject of an FBI investigation in 1958 due to the claims made by Reverend Bill Britton in a letter sent to J. Edgard Hoover, Director of the FBI. In this letter, Britton stated that Nelson was "using the FBI to authenticate his story of having gone to Venus, Mars, and the Moon in a fly saucer." According to Britton, Nelson said that he was taken by FBI agents from his farm to Washington D.C., for interrogation, and he gave a negative of a picture of these flying saucers. Also, Britton added that Nelson mentioned that the FBI forgave him for speaking about certain military secrets told to him by these "space brothers". He told this experience in a booklet that he sold for $1.00 apiece. Finally, in his letter, Britton pointed out several questions regarding Nelson's claims, being the most important question the one that asked: "Did you forbid him to speak of certain military secrets?"

Bill Britton and his wife Nadine in the early 1960's

It is important to note that most historians of the United States consider 1947 as the year when the Cold War began with the implementation of the "Truman Doctrine" to contain the propagation of world Communism, which gave rise to the anti-communist hysteria of the following years known as the Second Red Scare of the '50s. For the FBI, it wasn't so much whether or not the contactee's claims, like Buck Nelson, George Adamski, and others, were true. What bothered J. Edgar Hoover's Men in Black was the influence these people were having on the American public and their claims that they had military secrets. The problem with most of these contactees' claims was that these were not limited to Venusian encounters and flying UFOs. Behind this message was a matter of military secrets and national security. Today, these claims seem unimportant, but at the peak of the Cold War, they were serious business, a threat to national security. The loyalty of a group of citizens toward their government. As a result, the Hoover's Kid decided to take a closer look at this Ozark Mountain farmer.

The first three numbers of any FBI file designation indicate the kind of offense the FBI was investigating when it opened the file. For example, a file number that begins "025" would be classification 25, or an investigation into draft evasion or violation of the Selective Service Act. Nelson's file number begins with 43. This code number refers to:

> Illegal Wearing of Uniforms; False Advertising or Misuse of Names, Words, Emblems or Insignia; Illegal Manufacture, Use, Possession, or Sale of Emblems and Insignia; Illegal Manufacture, Possession, or Wearing of Civil Defense Insignia; Miscellaneous, Forging or Using Forged Certificate of Discharge from Military or Naval Service; Miscellaneous, Falsely Making or Forging Naval, Military, or Official Pass; Miscellaneous, Forging or Counterfeiting Seal of Department or Agency of the United States; Misuse of the Great Seal of the United States or of the Seals of the President or the Vice President of the United States; Unauthorized Use of "Johnny Horizon" Symbols. Unauthorized Use of Smokey Bear Symbol. Taken from: ago, Mari, Ana., Leon Andrew Immerman. (1981). *ARE YOU NOW OR HAVE YOU EVER BEEN IN THE FBI FILES. How to Secure and Interpret Your FBI Files.* GROVE Press Inc. New York: United States.

In popular culture and UFO conspiracy theories, Men in Black(MIB) are supposed to be men dressed in black suits who claim to be quasi-government agents or mysterious men working for unknown organizations or in various branches of government. The allegedly main task is protecting secrets or performing other strange activities with the mission to harass, threaten, retaliate or even assassinate unidentified flying objects (UFO) witnesses. In 1947, Harold Dahl claimed to have been warned not to talk about his alleged UFO sighting on Maury Island by a man in a dark suit. In the mid-1950s, ufologist Albert K. Bender claimed he was visited by men in dark suits who threatened and warned him not to continue investigating UFOs.

As a result of this FBI investigation on Nelson, FBI agents contacted him on March 28, 1958. During his interview, Nelson claimed that he had been in contact with government agents, but none of them identified themselves as being from the FBI. He told the agents that he could not identify the agents or the agency they represented. Nelson told the Interviewing Agents they were the only individuals to his knowledge that identified themselves as being from the FBI. He stated that he has never made statements to other people, verbally or written, that the FBI has interrogated him, nor has 'affiliated with him or his activities in any way. He stated that he has never been taken to Washington, D.C. for interrogation by the FBI or any other Government Agency; however, he has been in Washington, D. O. on , several occasions making speeches. He stated he has In his possession no military secrets and has never been forbidden by the U. S. Government to speak on his space travels, and undoubtedly stated that he is not a communist and does not believe in communism. Finally, Nelson was warned by the agents against involving the FBI in promoting his publications and activities.

Buck Nelson was a flamboyant contactee. He achieved some celebrity status as the guy who sold Venusian dog hair from his giant 385-pound dog, "Big Bo," and his trips to Mars, the Moon, and Venus, which he chronicled in a 1956 booklet with the same title, My Trip to Mars, the Moon, and Venus. In 1958 Nelson began hosting his own annual "Spacecraft Conventions" at his ranch in Mountain View, Missouri. In 1958 Nelson began hosting his own yearly "Spacecraft Conventions" at his farm in Mountain View, Missouri. Besides the typical bookstalls for lecturers' wares, Nelson had his saucer souvenir booth that sold toys, postcards, ball-point pens, pennants, balloons, liniment for sore backs, and more. Nelson also operated a concession stand offering such refreshments as hotdogs, burgers, and soda. By Nelson's final convention in 1966, attendance was down to 150 people, down from the phenomenal turnout of 1958 with about 2000 customers.

By his own words, as mentioned in *My Trip to Mars, the Moon, and Venus* (1956), Nelson worked most of his life as a laborer, leaving school after the sixth grade to work as a farmhand, and spent a good portion of his adult life traveling across the United States, taking a variety of jobs as he went, including as a logger, railroader, rancher, and farmer. Later in his life, Nelson purchased eighty acres in the Ozark Mountains of Missouri, near Mountain View, settling down to a farm and run a sawmill before his eventual retirement. Nelson purchased eighty acres in the Ozark Mountains of Missouri, near Mountain View, settling down to farm and run a sawmill before his eventual retirement.

Buck Nelson (April 9, 1895 - 1982) was an American farmer who claimed to have had an encounter with an unidentified flying object and its human crew in 1954 while living in Missouri. Buck Nelson believed the friendly occupants of the spacecraft to be humans from the planet Venus. His story is contained in a 1956 booklet he authored, *My Trip to Mars, the Moon, and Venus*. He told that that he saw three flying saucers over his farmhouse; he took photographs and attempted to signal with a flash-light. A beam of light "much brighter and hotter than the sun" was shined at him. Consequently, he testified that his chronic lumbago disappeared and his eyesight dramatically improved. He goes on to claim that, after dusk fell, three "friendly human spacemen" accompanied by a large dog, visited him and spent some time talking with him.

Nelson further stated that two of the people from Venus had adopted the names Bucky and Bob, and their main message concerned the "Twelve Laws of God", similar to the biblical Ten Commandments. He claimed to have been taken on trips to the Moon, Mars and Venus. He described how space people told him that on earth, past civilizations existed and destroyed themselves "They had learned of a power even greater than our Atomic power". He said the space people warned him that the inappropriate use of nuclear energy was threatening the earth again; "We are here to see which way this world will use Atomic power; for peace or war. We have stood by and seen other planets, one after another, destroy itself. Is this world next? We wonder and watch and wait. Again I say; give up your Atomic weapons and may Peace be on this Earth". Similarly to Moses, Nelson was also given Commandments. These are a set of biblical principles relating to ethics and worship.

After returning to his home planet, Nelson promised the aliens that he would tell everybody about his travels. He spoke to the media about his experiences and was supposedly questioned by the armed forces.

Nelson also described what he called a "book machine" thus "on Venus, Bucky managed to show me what I called a "Book Machine". When a book was put into it, it would read the pages, play any music or show any picture it contained. It was about the size of a television set".

James L. Hill of Seymour, Missouri and long friend of Nelson said that he looked different in appearance after the space brothers visited him in 1954. His face was white and his eyes looked as if he had seen a vision, Also, Hill claimed that Nelson's medical records at the hospital showed that he formerly had arthritis, and after the visit, Mr. Nelson made a marvelous recovery.

In 1956, Nelson published a booklet entitled: *My Trip to Mars, the Moon, and Venus,* and became something of a celebrity. He held a successful annual Spacecraft Convention near his 40-acre farm, seven miles northwest of Mountain View, in Howell County, in the Missouri Ozarks, each year since 1954, the first yearAt this event, he sold his pamphlet, and pay envelopes containing a small amounts of black hair, which he claimed had fallen off the large dog called "Bo".

Nelson died in 1982. An unconfirmed told that he was was once a police detective in the Los Angeles, Calif., Police Department.He spent his declining years with relatives in California. His story achieved a notable degree of popularity, but not that of other contactees such as George Adamski or Daniel Fry.

Buck Nelson led a fascinating life no matter what anyone thought of him. He never rose to prominence in UFO circles. We barely know anything about him except his FBI File and his own words. We can't know what was in his heart. We hope that we can learn more about him. The truth, whatever it is, should be told.

DEPARTMENT OF JUSTICE

FEDERAL BUREAU OF INVESTIGATION

BUCK NELSON

43-13592-424

MARCH 21, 1958-APRIL 2, 1958

March 21, 1958

REC-50 /3/3/3593- 413

EX-136 Reverend Bill Britton

b6
b7C

Dear Mr. Britton:

Your letter dated March 13, 1958, has been received while Mr. Hoover is out of the city, and I am acknowledging it for him.

I will bring your communication to his attention upon his return.

Sincerely yours,

Helen W. Gandy
Secretary

2 cc's - Kansas City, with two copies of incoming

ATTENTION SAC: Correspondent is not identifiable in Bufiles. On the basis of information furnished, the only reference in Bureau indices referring to Buck Nelson is Detroit memo dated 8-8-55, captioned "Detroit Flying Saucer Club, Espionage-X," copy furnished to your office.

An Agent of your office should contact Nelson immediately and determine the nature of data he is disseminating. He should be emphatically admonished against involving the FBI in promotion of his publications and activities. Advise the Bureau when action completed, forwarding a copy of the Mimeographed booklet in question, under caption "Reverend Bill Britton, Research (Crime Records)." Sulet no later than 4-2-58.

NOTE: (See next page)

DCL:cr
(6)

P.S. He claims scientists from Palomar visited him three times and verified his story. Do you have any knowledge of this?

Rep. Bob Sikes of Florida can verify that I have actively fought communism in Florida, and I think there is more to this Buck Nelson than appears on the surface.

Did you know he is planning a Convention in June with visitors from England + other lands, making plans for 10,000 — that NBC Radio is to carry this?

Eph. 3:8 "Preaching the Gospel of the Kingdom" II Cor. 4:5

Evangelist Bill Britton

March 13, 1958

J. Edgar Hoover, Director
Federal Bureau of Investigation
Washington, D.C.

Dear Sir:

I would like some information on a man by name of Buck Nelson of Mountain View, Missouri who is using the FBI to authenicate his story of having gone to Venus, Mars and the Moon in a flying saucer. He claims the FBI took him from his farm to Washington, D.C. for interrogation, and that they now have the negative of a picture he took of these flying saucers. He says that after failing to break down his story, you forbid him to speak of certain military secrets that the space brothers had told him of. He has a mimeographed booklet of his adventures he sells for $1.00 and mails out throughout the U.S. This booklet has been advertised over radio and T.V. as his true adventures, not fiction, and he uses your office as proof of its truth. If he is lying, it would seem to me that he is using the mails to defraud, for the book is interesting only if true, and many are ordering and buying it on that basis.

Would you please answer the following questions concerning this:

1. Did FBI agents visit Buck Nelson at his farm in Mtn View?
2. Did they take him to Washington for questioning?
3. Has he ever been questioned by the FBI concerning his space travels?
4. Did you forbid him to speak of certain military secrets?
5. Do you have the negative of his flying saucer snapshot?
6. Have you ever heard of Buck Nelson, or had him under investigation?
7. Do you have authenic proof of existence of space men or flying saucers?
8. Doesn't the fact that he uses the mails without penalty prove his story to be true? Otherwise, wouldn't he be defrauding the people?

Please answer, I have friends who are financially involved in this. Thank you,

Rev Bill Britton

Letter to:
    Reverend Bill Britton

NOTE: Bufile 65-63277 described the activities of the Detroit Flying Saucer Club, and Detroit advised in August, 1955, that Buck Nelson was the main speaker at one of this group's meetings at that time. He was described as being a 64-year-old farmer residing at Buck's Mountain View Ranch, located at, Mountain View, Missouri. No other background available. Detroit had received a complaint from an individual attending this meeting in that Nelson had stated "the form of Government under which we live in the U. S. is wrong and should be destroyed, along with all Government buildings." This citizen furnished a tape recording of certain statements of Nelson's which would indicate that he may be mentally unbalanced.

NORTH
Map to help you find my place.

- Mountain View
- Mt. Oliva Church
- "NN"
- Willow Springs
- Buck's Place
- 5 MILES
- "NN"
- U.S. 60
- Trask Road
- Houton Valley Road

WEST / EAST / SOUTH

Office Memorandum • UNITED STATES GOVERNMENT

TO : DIRECTOR, FBI
DATE: 4/2/58

FROM : SAC, KANSAS CITY (65-1544)

SUBJECT: REVEREND BILL BRITTON
RESEARCH (CRIME RECORDS)

OO: Kansas City

Unauthorized Use of Bureau Name

Reference Bureau letter to Reverend BILL BRITTON, Chanute, Kansas, dated 3/21/58.

On March 28, 1958, BUCK NELSON, Route 1, Mountain View, Missouri, was interviewed by Special Agents FRANK B. BUELL and LARRY C. BOYER. NELSON furnished identical information as contained in the miscellaneous literature he furnished the agents concerning his trip to Venus, Mars and the Moon, which literature is attached. NELSON stated he has been contacted on various occasions in the past by Government Agents; however, none of these agents ever identified themselves specifically as being with the FBI. He stated these agents were very helpful to him in planning lectures, and the disseminating of information he obtained on Venus, Mars and the Moon. He stated he could not identify any of these agents nor could he specifically identify the agency which they represented. NELSON advised the interviewing agents they were the only individuals to his knowledge that identified themselves as being from the FBI. He stated at no time has he ever made statements to other people, verbally or written, that the FBI has interrogated him, nor has affiliated with him or his activities, in any way. He stated at no time has he ever been taken to Washington, D.C. for interrogation by the FBI, or any other Government Agency; however, he has been in Washington, D.C. on several occasions making speeches. He stated he has in his possession no military secrets, and has never been forbidden by the U. S. Government to speak on his space travels. NELSON stated emphatically he is not a communist and does not believe in com-

REC-23   43-13592-424

② Bureau (Encl. 8)
1 Kansas City
FBB:slh
(3)

KC 65-1544

munism. He stated very emphatically he believes in God and the Bible.

NELSON was admonished against involving the FBI in promotion of his publications and activities. He stated he has not done this to date, and has no intention of ever doing it.

It is noted that prior to contacting NELSON, contact was made with Captain J.A. TANDY and Lieutenant G. KAHLER, Missouri State Highway Patrol, Willow Springs, Missouri. Both Captain TANDY and Lieutenant G. KAHLER verified the fact that NELSON is a "bug" on space travels, and has broadcast over local radio stations both in Willow Springs and other small stations throughout the country concerning his travels in space. Captain TANDY stated it is the consensus of opinion of the local population that NELSON is a "crackpot." TANDY stated that NELSON is having a convention in June, 1958, and it is expected that "possibly several thousand" persons will attend, the "Saucer Clubs" have large followings.

It appeared to the interviewing agents that NELSON is a senile man who is very sincere in his statements of outer space, and who definitely believes he has made a trip to outer space.

The following is a description of NELSON as obtained from observation and interrogation:

Name:	BUCK NELSON
Race:	White
Sex:	Male
Age:	62
DOB:	4/9/95, at Denver, Colorado
Height:	5' 6"
Weight:	135 pounds
Scars and Marks:	None
Hair:	Gray
Eyes:	Blue
Marital Status:	Single
Relatives:	None
Residence:	Route 1, Mountain View, Missouri (residence called Buck's Mountain View Ranch; however, it is a very small four room house, built

- 2 -

KC 65-1544

> by NELSON and located in the "back hills" approximately 10 - 12 miles from Mountain View, Missouri)

No further investigation is being conducted and this matter is being closed UACB.

To The Bureau 8 Enclosures

KC 45-1344

Re: REVEREND BILL BRITTON
RESEARCH (CRIME RECORDS)

(1) Two membership cards to Buck's Flying Saucer Club.

(2) One letterhead, Buck's Mountain View Ranch.

(3) Two leaflets entitled Spacecraft Convention.

(4) Two leaflets entitled My Trip To Mars The Moon and Venus.

(5) One book entitled My Trip to Mars the Moon and Venus by Buck Nelson.

43-13592-424

"My Trip to Mars, the Moon, and Venus" — No Fiction - Its True! - $1.00 plus tax and postage

Buck's Mountain View Ranch
BUCK NELSON
Route 1 - Mountain View, Missouri

TEXT ON THIS PAGE IS ILLEGIBLE
WE HAVE LEFT THE PAGE AS REFERENCE

FLYING SAUCER CLUB

THIS IS TO CERTIFY THAT—

_____

IS A LIFE MEMBER OF
BUCK'S FLYING SAUCER CLUB

DATE_____195___

FLYING SAUCER CLUB

THIS IS TO CERTIFY THAT—

_____

IS A LIFE MEMBER OF
BUCK'S FLYING SAUCER CLUB

DATE_____195___

"My Trip to Mars, the Moon and Venus"

You will find this booklet very interesting, and you will be THRILLED by the first hand physical experiences of this Ozark Mountain Farmer. A True Story that will appeal to both old and young.

Read about his life. Read of life on other planets!

Simple Statement of Facts!
No Fiction - It's True!

BY

BUCK NELSON

• • •

A Farmer...
Describes
His
Flying
Saucers

• • •

Speaks With People from Outer Space

Price $1.05 Tax and Postage Paid

Use reverse side as an order blank — Please Print

MAIL YOUR ORDER TO:

Buck's Mountain View Ranch

BUCK NELSON, RT. 1, MOUNTAIN VIEW, MO.

SPACECRAFT
Convention

Speeches and Discussions
PICNIC
PROGRAM STARTS 10 A.M. SATURDAY

SPREAD THE WORD
PUBLIC INVITED

COME and bring as many people as possible

HEAR SPEAKERS WHO HAVE CONTACTED OUR SPACE BROTHERS

Do Not Miss This
BIG EVENT

ADMISSION FREE — — FREE CAMPING

Bring your own tent, house car or camping outfit, your own food water, folding chairs, sleeping bags, etc.

NOT RESPONSIBLE FOR ACCIDENTS

June 28-29, 1958
AT
BUCK'S MOUNTAIN VIEW RANCH

BUCK NELSON, ROUTE 1

MOUNTAIN VIEW, MISSOURI

MY TRIP TO MARS, THE MOON, AND VENUS

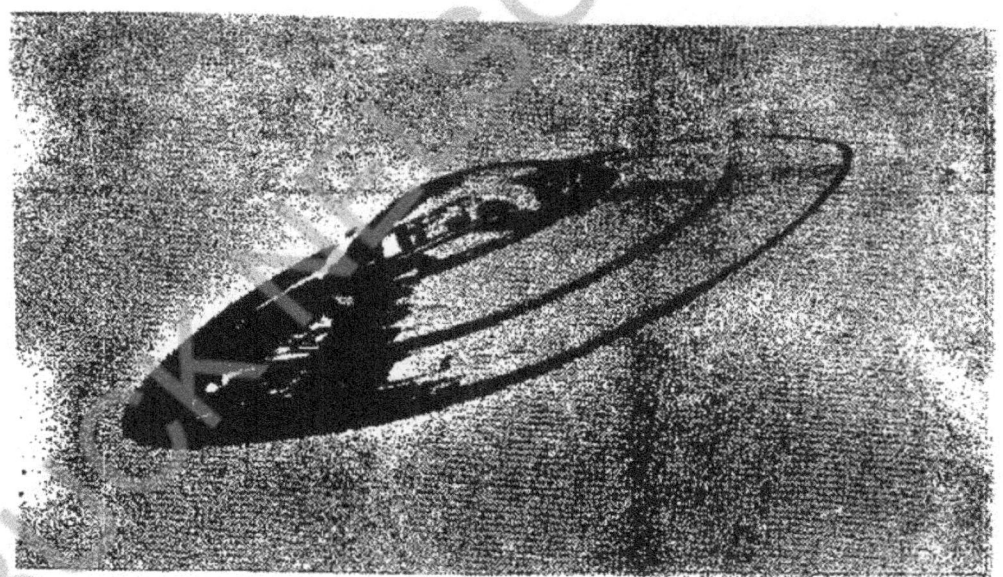

by BUCK NELSON

MY TRIP TO MARS, THE MOON AND VENUS

BY
BUCK NELSON

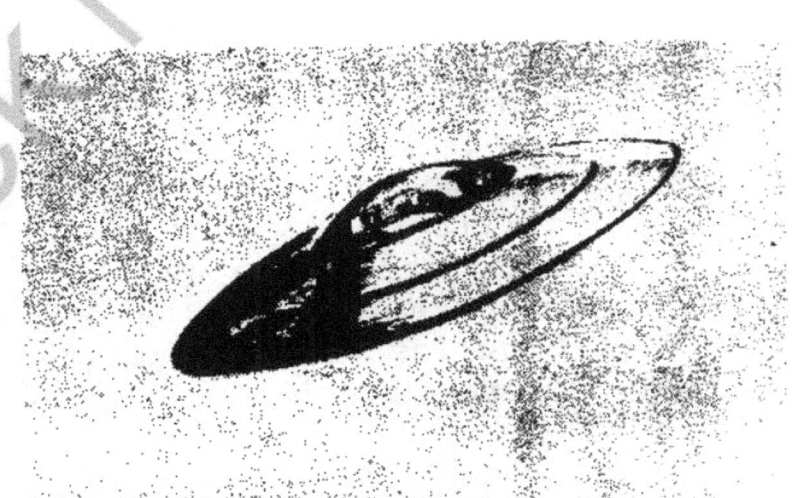

DEDICATION

I dedicate this book to

Mr. and Mrs. Sherman Lowery

of

Clarkston Michigan

BUCK NELSON

ACKNOWLEDGEMENTS

I wish to express my deep appreciation and thanks to all those whose encouragement has helped make this booklet possible; To the Lowery's for their home, Nathan Riffle and many others who have so willingly assisted me. Also many thanks go out to the Grand Rapids Flying Saucer Club for the first printing of this booklet.

December 1956   Buck Nelson

BUCK NELSON

A WORD ABOUT THE AUTHOR

I will give my readers a brief summary of my life.

I was born near Denver, Colorado, April, 9, 1895. I have spent most of my life on a farm and large cattle ranches. I only managed to get a sixth grade education at school.

I have worked as a top hand on many central western cattle ranches when very young. I have logged and run a saw mill of my own, making, both lumber and railroad ties. I have railroaded, worked as a special policeman, farmed, run an auto park etc.

I have traveled in all of our forty eight good old states of the U.S.A. and many foreign lands. After tiring of it all, I longed for the farm again. I purchased eighty acres in the Ozark Mountains of Missouri, twelve and one half miles from the nearest town, Mountain View, Missouri.

Here I farmed some and I bought a saw mill and made lumber and railroad ties. after a few years, old ailments and age got the best of me and I retired. --- lucky to have my Ozark Mt. Home.

As you will read in my story, the Flying Saucers first appeared over my Ozark Mountain home July 30, 1954. I wrote of the experience to the Springfield Missouri newspaper. They printed it in their daily paper. As I have had no experience as a writer or a lecturer, I intended to drop the whole thing right there and forget it all.

Then, Mr. James L. Hill of Seymour Missouri, (Route 2); World War Veteran, read the article in the paper. Mr. Hill thought the world should know about my experience and mailed a copy of the paper to Flying Saucer Clubs in the East. I was investigated by several in the East, and I was called to lecture to the public and tell my story on the stage at halls, churches and schools.

So the world and I are indebted to Mr. James L. Hill; also George Adamski has done much to help me, and he tells the world that he believes my story. Now I am thankful that my story was not dropped right there and forgotten, as I since have had many contacts with space men, and my trip to Mars, the Moon and Venus, for which I will ever be thankful. So I must stop here and let my readers read my story.

Every bit of it is TRUE....

BUCK NELSON

FOREWORD

Friends; the reason that I, a housewife and seamstress am introducing Mr. Buck Nelson is because I believe I know him better than any one outside of his friends and neighbors at his home. Some Air Force officials have been to see him so many times that they know him fairly well, but they are not allowed to talk about his experiences very much, if at all.

The experience of Mr. Nelson can fairly stagger the mind of even those of us who have studied the laws of Ontology. However, if you think of him as a person whose work is similar to that of JOHN the BAPTIST, foretelling the coming of a great teacher; then it isn't too hard to take.

If a person has had a great deal of training along some certain lines of science, then it is practically impossible for him to believe that Mr. Nelson's trip was taken in the flesh, and wasn't just a soul flight. For example, ...the speed at which the interplanetary ships travel makes it impossible to fit the whole idea of them into the framework of our own methods of locomotion. Even rockets cannot be compared to them. It is necessary to be able to conceive of there being an entirely different method of moving about. These interplanetary ships use magnetic power and are almost soundless. They use lines of energy which exist between the Sun and the planets just as there are lines of energy from a magnet and a piece of steel, which are held apart by a counter pull of some kind or are fixed apart.

vii

The Space Folks tell us that they can come into our atmosphere at any time, but can leave better at midnight. The moon also affects their traveling the same as it affects our tides. They travel with nature instead of blasting through it.

In telling of his trip to Mars, the moon, and Venus, Mr. Nelson tells you only what he perceived with the five senses. Each one of you can evaluate it in comparison with anything in which you are most interested.

When 'Little Bucky of Venus' visited Mr. Nelson on Christmas day, 1955, he tells him some things which are prevalent on other planets. Conditions which we should work toward, if we are ever to make a start toward that kind of life which Jesus taught us to pray for when He gave us the Lords Prayer. That Heavenly condition must be attainable or else we would not be taught to pray that the will of the Father should be done on earth as it is in Heaven. Surely Jesus would not teach us to ask for that which we could never possess.

--- --- ---

When Mr. Nelson first saw the saucers, especially the lowest one, he wondered what the thing was and immediately named it " The Thing". The local papers and farm magazine which he took, did not print anything about the Saucers, so he hadn't the slightest idea what they were. He has been accused of making up the story of his experience from Saucer books but he did not have even one Saucer book at that time. I know this, because I sent him the Saucer books myself and that was long after the time of his experience.

George Adamski sent Mr. Nelson a copy of "Flying Saucers Have Landed", but it came up missing on the very day that he received it. He proudly displayed, " Inside the Space Ships ", which he had just received from Mr. Adamski, to my sister and me. Mr. Nelson's experience happened while this second book was yet in the publisher's hands, and he couldn't have gotten it if he had known about it, which he did not.

On October 4th, 1955, my sister Florence Collins and I visited Buck. On the 26th of December my son Nathan Riffle and I arrived at his place at Mountain View, Missouri. Just about 15 hours earlier the space man, " Little Bucky ", had left. We stayed until the afternoon of the 29th of December, 1955.

My third visit was made with my husband Sherman, while Buck was in Washington, D.C. Our intention had been to stay down at Mountain View for a week and then bring Buck back with us, as many people in Michigan, especially Grand Rapids, after having heard him talk in Detroit, wished to have him return to lecture again.

On the 21st of June, which was during our stay at Buck's ranch, we had what we called a 'space' picnic. Our guests were, Mr. and Mrs. Tedrick, from Westplains, Missouri; Mr. and Mrs. Christen, who live on a lovely farm a few miles from Buck's place; and Mr. and Mrs. James Hill of Seymour, Missouri. The Hill's are two of the people that saw the Space Ships on the day they first came down low on Buck's place.

We surely wished that some of the space folks would join our picnic but the only interplanetary traveler we had with us was Teddy, Buck's little dog. I was reading Bucky's "Christmas Message", aloud, in a voice as much like the space man's as I possibly could. Teddy was lying in the grass after having been well fed, and as soon as I started reading in Buck's tone of voice, he jumped up and ran around the couch where I was sitting and looked up in my face all the time I was reading.
I felt sorry for him, he surely must have thought his space man friend had returned. He loved Bucky so very much.

We didn't know until Buck Nelson arrived at our place in Clarkston, Michigan on July 2nd, that the Space Brothers had been taking a peek at us at that picnic.

Buck told us that Bucky's voice had broken in on a radio program when he was "in his room" at Washington, D.C. Bucky had told him that there was quite a gathering of people in his yard and there was plenty of feed for the horse and colt in the barrels and that they were well cared for.

Ancient and modern history as well as the Bible record the visits of Space People to our planet. Indian legends are another source of this same type of information.

But now folks, the most wonderful thing is that one of our own neighbors, Buck Nelson, has actually made a trip to other planets and will now tell you about it. It is with both pride and humility that my husband, Sherman and I, had Buck Nelson of the Ozarks as our guest for the greater part of the month of July, 1956. So now folks, Mr. Buck Nelson, of Mountain View Ranch, Mountain View, Missouri.

December 1956   FANNY LOWERY

MY TRIP

to Mars, the MOON and VENUS

The First Contact

The first part of my story started on July 30th, 1954. I was listening to my radio at my home at four o'clock in the afternoon, when it began to go crazy wild. My dog, too, set up a barking and my pony outside began to raise all kinds of cain. I went outside to see what my animals were doing.

As I went out the kitchen door, right over head was a huge disc-like object. High in the big heavens were two more. I went back in to get my camera and I returned and photographed them 3 times. However, when the pictures came back from being developed and printed, only one picture showed two of the (what I called) "Things" (for want of a better name). I had never heard of " Flying Saucers ".

I dont know why, but when I went back to the house to get the camera, I had picked up the flashlight. Anyway, I waved the flashlight at these "Things", as a signal for them to come down and land. Instead of them coming down, they shot some kind of a ray at me. It was much brighter and hotter than the sun. I certainly couldn't have stood it if it had lasted a few seconds longer.

The ray knocked me down behind a barrel, and I waited until these "Things" had left before I tried to get up, as it was very hard for me to get up. I had suffered, off and on, from lumbago in my back, and neuritis in my side and arm, for fifteen years. When I started to get up, easy-like, I was surprised because I felt no pain. Now regardless of how bad the weather is or how cold, there is no pain in my back. The ray also helped my eyes, so that, although my eyesight isn't perfect I no longer need to wear glasses, even to read, although I wore them for many years before. That was my first contact and it took place at about four o'clock on the afternoon of July 30th, 1954.

The Second Contact

The second contact came six months later, on February 1st, 1955 at 12 noon. This time they circled low over the house and asked in a friendly voice, whether I was friendly or not. It was some kind of public address system, I think. They said they would like to land in the back of my pasture, beyond the house, where there is a spring. They wanted to know if I would allow them to land unmolested, many times if necessary.

They did not land this time, and talked for only a few minutes. Then they bid me good-bye, and said, "we'll see you again".

The Third Contact

A little over a month went by. Then on March 5th, 1955, about midnight, they landed and came up to the house. There were three men and a huge dog. One of them was a young earth-man who had gone to Venus two years before this. He was called "Little Buck" or "Bucky".

The next man was a trainee, I was told, who was learning to operate the space ship. The fact that he was old and wrinkled didn't seem to matter. Though he was friendly and interested, he did not

- 2 -

speak or tell his name. Then there was one fellow called Bob Solomon. I was later told he was 200 years old, but he didn't look any older than little Bucky, who was nineteen. Last, but not least, was the big dog, "Bo". He put up his paw to shake hands just as the men had. When I later saw him stand on his hind legs, he was higher than my head. I also found out that he weighed 385 pounds.

They stayed with me for about one hour. They were interested in everything in and about the house. They compared their things with mine and showed me how theirs made less work. My bed, for instance, had dust under it. As I'm a bachelor and more interested in my animals than dust under the bed. They told me, and later I saw, how their beds were built half into the wall. There were no blankets or sheets to wash, nor even bed making to do. A sort of canopy came down over the bed for privacy and dials could be set for your comfort. Even the pillow was part of the mattress. The feel of it made it seem similar to foam rubber with a soft, smooth washable surface. All this, they explained to me, made less work, and a more comfortable home.

I built a fire in the woodstove, to show the spacemen and also lit the oilstove. Bob Solomon just about burned his hand on it. He thought it was not hot. They wanted to know about the radio, especially the battery on top of it. When I told them that the battery was for power, they waved their hands over their heads and said, "What, with all of this power overhead, and you use that"? Then they shook their heads. I have a little electric light plant that makes my electric current for lights, etc. The spacemen wanted to see it run. They wanted to know _why_ I needed it. They said they plugged their lights and appliances into their radio for power.

They were interested in everything I had in my home and asked me about this and that. They passed up a picture of Christ and other Christian pictures on the wall. I asked them if they did not mean anything to them and one remarked,"Yes, we understand, but you people dont". They said we have an entire misconception of it all. When they were in the house on this visit they had told me I could go on a trip to other planets if I would tell about it to the world. They left after being with me for about an hour.

The Fourth Contact

On March 22nd, 1955 at about 12 midnight, they circled low over the house. They did not land. They visited some and told me to get ready for my trip into space.

Down back of the house are three springs which the spacemen cleaned out. They asked permission to get water at them any time they wished. I was more than glad to let them get it. At some time when they had been there, they had placed 12 rocks in a circle. It was too little for a flower bed, and was not in the right place anyway. It was near where the space ships land. I later asked the spacemen if they had placed the rocks there in the circle. They said that they had, and that it was a symbol of the 12 laws of God, which are also their only laws.

The Fifth Contact

When my friends came after me on April 24th, 1955 at midnight, for my trip into space, it did not take long to get ready to go. I was asked to put on a clean pair of overalls that the laundry had just washed, that the spacemen saw hanging near. I was asked to put them on, as there would be nothing in the pockets. I was told that anything that I took along would be magnetized, so could not take my watch. I left milk out for my cat, which I call "Krazy", and Trixie, my horse, could get feed out on the range. Ted, my dog, went on this trip with me. I could hardly wait to get down back to the place where the ship had landed.

Before I was asked to enter the ship, I was told I could write down the 12 laws of God I had asked about. I was told I could take a tablet and a pencil along to take notes. So I was asked to sit on a rock outside of the ship and write down the twelve laws of God by the light of the open spaceship door and the light of the stars. After I had copied the laws down, word for word as they were given to me, I was asked if it meant anything to me to write down the Laws of God outside under the stars. I replied that perhaps it was close to nature, and they asked, "and God"? I said "Yes".

So here are the laws as they were given to me........

THE TWELVE LAWS OF GOD...ON VENUS

(These twelve laws were given to Buck Nelson, at his farm at Mountain View, Missouri, on April 24th, 1955, by men from the planet Venus. These laws are followed faithfully, and are not just something to mention occasionally.)

LOVE: Love your Maker, your parents, your neighbor, all birds and animals of the earth, and everything in the sea and air.

HONOR: Honor your God and parents. Obey God's law which is also man's law.

OBEY: Obey God's law, your parents and the rights of others.

THE LAWS
1. Love your Maker... God.

2. Thou shalt not kill... includes accidents and war.
3. Love your neighbor.
4. Let your light shine before men, and all will see your good works, and it will be an honor to you and your Maker... God.

5. Thou shalt not commit adultery.

6. Thou shalt not steal.

7. Thou must do as thou wish to be done by.

8. No other god shall be before thee.

9. Do not take the name of God in vain.

10. Honor your father and mother.

11. Your body is God's; do not misuse it in any way. Do not drink or eat anything that is not food. Use nothing to harm the body, either inside or out. Wear nothing on the body that harms it or is of no use.

12. God made the heaven and the earth and we must give Him thanks for what he gives us.

With these TWELVE LAWS of GOD, and the rules governing them, all enclosed in a Bible of some 20 pages, the people of the other planets in our solar system are able to live in an order without wars; without armed forces or police; without tobacco, coffee or tea; without liquor and harmful drugs; from the use of unrefined natural foods, disease is very rare, hence no hospitals, no prisons or sanitarium; The span of life is greatly extended, the cost of government is very small, the rule being based on truth and justice.

After I had written the 12 laws down, the spacemen gave their dog, "Big Bo", a bath in the spring and then my dog got a bath.

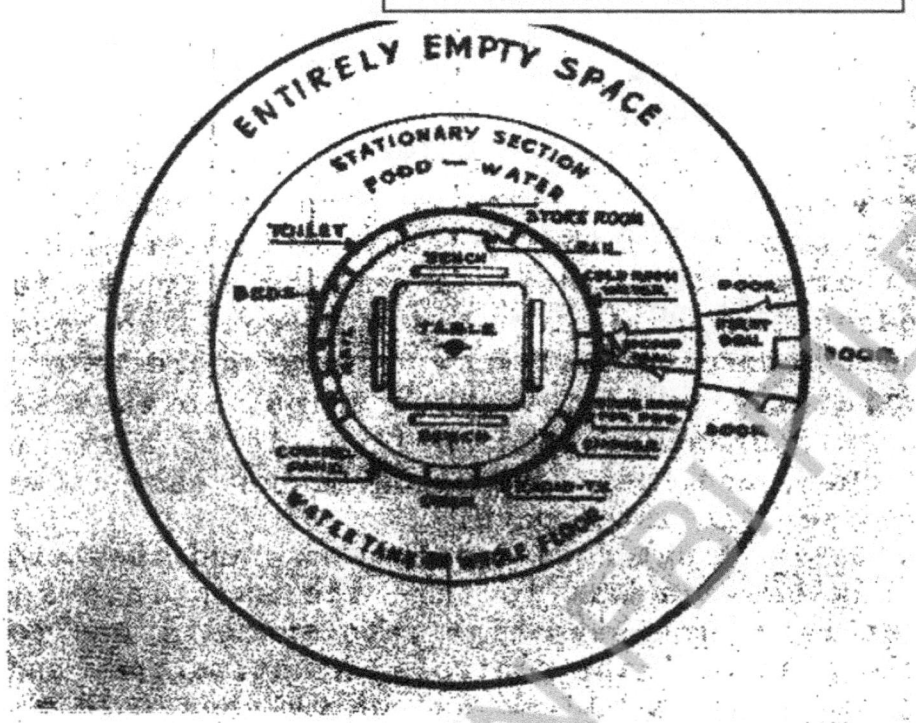

Floor plan of the interior of Spaceship
In which Buck Nelson Traveled

Details of Main Control Panel of Ship

Then I was invited into the ship. It was a wonderful experience, merely to enter such a ship. I was told I could take the ship up, and to sit at the control panel. Well, I sure did not feel capable of that.. I could drive a car, or a truck, but my goodness, a beautiful ship that could go from one planet to another...I knew it sure would take a lot of training to fly even our ships, so they saw my hesitation and assured me it would be alright, to sit down, and they would show me how easy it was to take the ship into space.

I sat down freely then, and they showed me how easy it was to take the ship into space. After I got the ship high into space, I was told I could play with the controls. Meantime they had put safety belts on all of us, which they told me was for the first time in three years. It was a good thing too, for I had the ship upside down and every which way. I punched every button I could see and turned every dial. I got results one way or the other from everything I touched. When I got the ship upside down, I got no help, only lots of laughs from the spacemen. When I got in trouble and I found what I did wrong, the opposite usually righted it. I was told that there was nothing I could do that would harm the ship or us.

I turned radio and T.V. controls thinking they were ship controls. I got results and ship to-ship operation I had lots of fun. If you are wondering what was happening to the two dogs while all this stuff was going on, well I'll tell you... Bucky was well aware of what would probably happen and Big Bo had a cage for just such an emergency. There was a spare cage for an extra dog, but Teddy was frightened and jumped up on Bucky's lap. The ship was perfectly steady when I wasnt at the controls. I think Big Bo enjoyed the sway of the ship caused by my playing with it.

When we first entered the ship, gauges

were set that control the air pressure so that it was adjusted to correspond to the air pressure on Mars, our next stop. Lights were turned out once to show me that it was inky black in space,

MARS

It seemed to be necessary to sleep when in space. Bucky woke me up and said we were just about to land on Mars.

Before we landed though, the ship tilted so that I could see the canal system... they wanted to show me that... After we got closer, the ship was tilted again to show me horses and cattle in the field. Finally we landed about 20 feet from the door of what I was told was a 'rulers home'. A good meal was ready for us; we ate, and the crew exchanged papers. My little dog, Teddy, was given a good meal of fish that he sure loved.

This building, which we entered, was built of rock on the outside, which I was told came from our moon. The interior seemed to be covered with steel of some kind. The part of the hinges which we would put onto a door with screws was moulded right into the door. The only small separate part of what to us would be the hinges, was the pin. A large diamond topped one of these pins.

The people there didn't know I was from earth until I was introduced as an Earth-man. The children came around then to ask questions. I was told that there are other races and colors of people there, but that I was taken where the people were most like the ones I was used to.

Mars is very colorful. I couldn't tell where one color ended and another began.

The people on Mars used solar and electric power.

The Light and Dark Sides of the Moon

We got back into the space ship and the gauges were set, this time to gradually get the ship ready for the moon's pressure.

Our next stop was on the light side of the moon. Again we went to the ruler's home and we ate a meal there. This ruler's home was built in a crater. The first room we entered seemed to be right next to the ruler's home. It had a telescope. There were shelves, which were both open and glass enclosed and tables holding rock samples. The quarries on the moon furnish rock for buildings on other very old planets where the surface has disintegrated into soil. There wasnt any vegetation on the light side or earth side of the moon. The water in the homes could have come from the snow on the mountains. These homes were clustered around huge hangars used for a base. I was told, for interplanetary travel. The earth is the only planet in the solar system which does not travel from one planet to another.

I was told that there are rivers and lakes on the dark side (the side away from the earth) of the moon, but I didnt see them when we stopped there because it was very hazy, but I could see the mountains. They were very high. On this second stop on the moon, we ate again. Although we had just eaten a meal at the first stop, we did full justice to it too. Plenty of food and sleep seemed to be necessary
There seemed to be a little more time to look about on the moon than there was on Mars or on Venus. I was allowed to walk outside and look about a little. I took a good look at a building so that I wouldn't get lost, as I was in strange territory, but Big Bo, the space man's dog, went with Teddy and me. The spacemen had not directed Bo to go with us, not in words

- 10 -

anyway, but I felt he was taking care of us. Children played with several sized dogs. They rode Big Bo like a pony and he would play with them, too.

VENUS

Again we took off in our spaceship, and some time later we landed on Venus. A watch would have been magnetized, so it would have been of no use on the trip or afterward. I simply lost all track of time, so I had no idea how much later it was when we landed on Venus.

On Venus we again made two stops. Each time was at a ruler's home. I saw three moons and it was just about as light as day on earth, though hazy and cloudy.

The homes were also built of rock with steel-like interiors.

A BUILDING ON VENUS

(Probably an Industrial Building)

The ruler at one stop was painting and wore overalls. His overalls didn't have all of the buckles and hooks which ours do and they were made of a different material.

At one of the stops on Venus there were three cars parked near the house which we entered. These cars looked a good bit like our new ones, except that they had no wheels or fenders. They skim along 3 to 5 feet off the ground and are powered the same as the space ships. They are not made to go out into space. They are made to be used just as we use a car. Having this type of car eliminates the need for roads. No roads, no police force, no jails, no government buildings and no wars. It isn't hard to understand why their taxes compare to ours like a nickel compares to a hundred dollars. When I started connecting this saving to the fact that the things they use are built to last forever so much longer than ours and that sickness is almost unknown, then it wasn't so hard to understand why they work only about an hour a day and never more than three hours.

Even housework, the spacemen told me- requires no more than one to three hours. This leaves plenty of leisure time for visiting and they do plenty of that. They really live by the laws of God.

Though we only stayed a possible 20 minutes at each stop on Venus, Bucky managed to show me what I called a "Book Machine". When a book was put into it, it would read the page, play any music or show any picture it contained . It was about the size of a television set.

At each of the two homes on Venus was a clock showing a face of 17 numerals. The numerals had sort of the general appearance of Chinese writing, but I am more inclined to think of them as hen scratchings. Since I was allowed only writing material with me on the trip, I couldn't photograph anything so I drew a picture of the face of the clock. They told me there were 17 hours a day and 17 hours a night and that their hours compared favorably with ours.

CLOCK ON VENUS

(Notice Seventeen Hour Day and
Seventeen Hour Night)

We ate a meal at both stops on Venus, though here again, as on the moon, the time was very short between stops. The food consisted of meat, milk, eggs, fish, many kinds of salads and also many cooked vegetables. I recognized corn positively, because it was not broken up in the cooking.

Though we slept a great deal while traveling, the space men talked to me also and told me about the way of life on other planets.

- 13 -

As folks here on earth ask me questions, it helps me recall things these space men told me. Also it helps me to recall some of the things which occured. For the sake of brevity, just the answers to some of the many questions will be given here.

I guess we had better come back to earth first. Our return to earth actually occured at midnight on April 27, 1955. After returning home, I caught the day of the week from the radio, but I had to get the date from the calendar at the bank in Mountain View, where only one day at a time is shown. I was so surprised that I had been away such a short time, I couldnt believe it.

I asked the banker if that was the right date and he sure gave me a funny look, but he answered me that it was correct. I had been away three days, two nights and two half nights.

QUESTIONS ANSWERED

Folks on Mars, the Moon and Venus look like us here on Earth, but are much better looking in general. They dress more simply as they dont use ties, buckles, beads, bangles, ear rings or bracelets, etc. Nothing is worn which restricts the body in any way. One of their Twelve Laws of God governs this. Men wore an overall type of pants without the buckles and studs which we have on ours. The material was different from our overalls.

They ate some meat. At least what I had looked and tasted like meat. Their food seemed to consist mainly of fruits and vegetables. They were healthy, happy people. I was told that disease is rare and as far as I could see, they had nice teeth.

I have asked about health and cures for diseases, as I know that is something that everyone wants to know about. They just told me they live the Laws of God. They don't have doctors as we know them. They are their own doctors and use what I would call natural medicines, if they are occasionally needed. They gave me a milkweed kind of lotion to use as I had a rash on my body from the change of water.

One thing they told me was that on earth we should use hypnotism to stop pain, and that it should never be used for entertainment.

Neither do they approve of competitive sports because they cause a strain on the whole body and especially the heart.

The folks I talked to spoke English very well. It seems that they learn the language of the people they will be contacting. They have told me that there are many of them amongst us. They have even taken some of our government officials up in their ships, but the officials are afraid to tell

- 15 -

about it for they have too much to lose. I have no family to suffer for what might happen to me.

I cannot say that I have been threatened, but I was offered a check for one thousand dollars if I would never tell my story again. A thousand dollars would have meant a lot up here in the mountains, but I don't want any money that is obtained in any such way as that.

One of the things that people here on Earth find so hard to accept, is the idea of space men coming to such a humble person as myself. And another is why they should come to such an isolated spot as my ranch. That has been their need. We would shoot them down, no doubt and try to ask questions afterwards. Another reason they come to my place, or rather this part of the country is that the magnetic currents are just right here. (This is a section of the country where there are caves; it might mean something to a scientist).

The space men tell me that the places where the magnetic currents cross, is comparable to a cross roads sign. These currents or lines of force are named and numbered. The moon has an effect on their travel also. I suppose that might be when they are near here, but really I don't know. They didn't tell me just how far the moon's effects reach. The technicalities and distances would not have meant much to me anyhow.

They landed many times at my place, but I only knew of this later when I would find a stone laid on top of a post or some such thing.

If I happen to see it, I can tell when a space ship is close, from the whirl of a magnet, which is suspended from the ceiling in my house. I have seen it whirl many times, but I never tried to contact them as I had promised them that I wouldn't bother them in any way.

The space ship itself is something to see. It is about 50 feet across and possibly 8 feet high. These ships can land or take off straight up or down and can come into our atmosphere at any time but can leave our atmosphere best at midnight. They can hover without landing also.

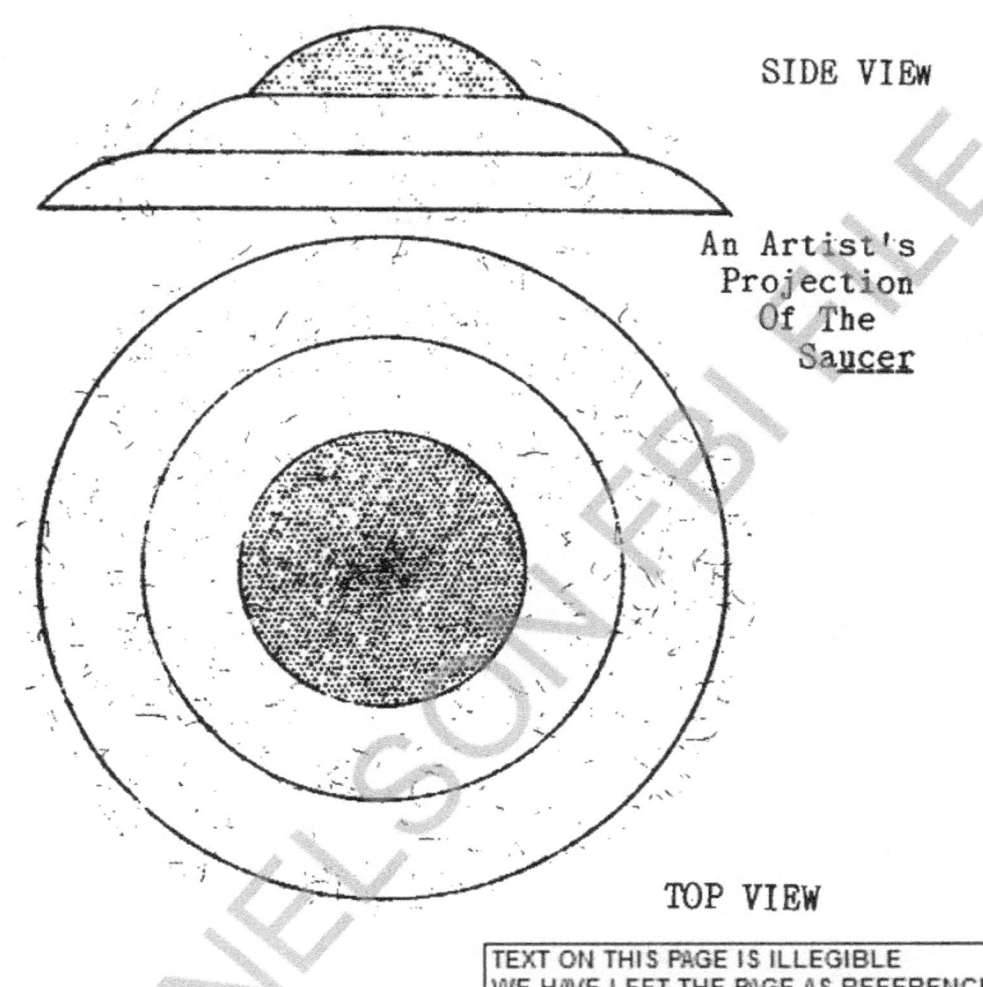

SIDE VIEW

An Artist's Projection Of The Saucer

TOP VIEW

The ship I was in did not go into a carrier ship or 'Mother Ship' such as I have read about since my trip. It traveled between planets on its own power. It had a raised center section which looked like glass. It was smooth, though and was raised like a blister, not with straight sides and then a dome. The edges were thin, rising gradually to the high center. To change direction in motion only the center section had to be turned. This is one reason they can dart about so fast. The ship goes by automatic control as well as by being piloted. It was perfectly steady when I wasn't playing with it.

Space here doesn't allow too much of a description of the inside of the ship nor details of the graphs used for the automatic control, but there is really no reason for me _not_ to tell them.

The very center of the ship has a very large table in it. I guess it must have been quite strong because their great big dog, Bo, got up on it. My dog Teddy was just at the edge of it but on the floor and I was telling him to roll over, sit up and beg. Big Bo was too large to roll on the table but he was obeying all the other commands I gave Teddy. Then he would hold his paws up and look around and laugh. It was plain as anything that he was saying, with everything he had to say it, "Look at me". "I can do it too". Bucky said that this was the first time Big Bo had ever obeyed commands given to another dog. Knowing my love for animals, Bucky allowed me to take a picture of him. In this picture you have to hunt for his eyes as his long hair hangs in clusters and is very shaggy in appearance. Actually it is fine and silky. Analysis has proved it to be hair from a male dog; a fine well bred, outdoor animal. The hair is hollow.

I have been asked whether I might have been taken to some other part of the earth on a ship made here on our earth. This would hardly be possible as the governments are too closely watched by each other to have such a wonderful ship. I dont think our scientists have yet mastered the things they would have to know in order to build such a ship. It is difficult for the space people to find words in our language which can be used to explain their methods of travel and type of power.

The government of these people on other planets seems to be very simple. They called it "home life". Actually, living according to the _Golden_ _Rule_ and _The_ _Twelve_ _Laws_ of _God_, eliminates the need for great government buildings, munitions, armies, police forces and jails.

Some of our commonly used methods of making a living would be absolutely unacceptable to them. One of these methods is our practice of making money from money in so many different ways.

They have a medium of exchange, but I was not told what it was. I doubt that it is gold. They told me that we bury our gold down in Kentucky, but that they use their gold around their homes, because the vibrations of gold are good for the body. That's one reason Colorado is such a healthy place.

If we will accept the people of other planets, they will accept us and show us how to live less troubled lives. They will also show us how to keep our planet from further tilting.

If we have a major disaster, that is one comparable to our Biblical Flood, they will help the ones here who accept them as brothers. They cannot do so otherwise. I think they know who these people are.

They certainly do use mental telepathy, but not to the extent that they don't use their voices for communication. Some of them do have an accent, just as most of us would if we learned a new language. This accent is quite noticable in a tape recording which Bucky made at my house on Christmas day 1955.

Bucky is a young earth man who was born in Colorado and was taken to Venus when he was 17 years old. (At the time, March 5th, that they came in the house, he had been gone about 2 years). I would say that he is about 21 years old now (1956).

When he was about 4 years old the space people came to his parents and invited them to go to Venus. The parents did not want to go themselves, but they agreed to bring Bucky up so that he could do the work which he is now doing. The way of life of the contacted people has to be just right. Bucky teaches English on Venus.

When Bucky and I got to checking up, we discovered that we were distant cousins. Bucky told me many things about my ancestors which I had never known before. Checking gave me proof that they were so. We also look something alike and Mrs. Lowery seemed to think that there was a slight similarity in our voices although Bucky's is higher in pitch and has an accent like a person from one of the Scandinavian countries.

When the space men shot the ray at me and cured my aching back, they did it to help me and also to pay me in part, in advance, for what they wished me to do for them. When they came into my house to visit me, I think they exerted just a little influence on my mind.

It was like this...

I wanted to see their ship. I wanted to ride in it and I wanted to go to their planet. This was after they had told me about their way of life being better than ours. I asked them if I could see their ship and they wouldn't answer me. I asked if I could ride in it and they wouldnt answer. Now I sure wouldn't have had the nerve to ask if I could go to their planet when they hadn't answered my first question, unless they had used this influence I spoke of, because I did ask if I could go. It seemed necessary to ask. They told me I could go if I would tell the public about it afterwards. This I have done to the best of my ability.

The hardest thing I ever had to do was to come back here and try to get along under the primitive conditions which we have here in these hills. This is a beautiful, heavily wooded mountain country but water is very often a major problem. Many people including myself, use filtered rain water. My spring which is the one where the space men got water, goes nearly dry at times.

The land is rocky and hard to work and the wood ticks seem to enjoy blood more than wood. Everything around the place and even large areas of

- 20 -

the yard have to be sprayed to keep them down. The ticks, along with the chiggers, etc, are the reason the dogs were washed in the spring before we went on the trip. After we got on the ship, the three men and I took a bath. I dont think they would have cared much about having ticks for visitors. I'm afraid the ticks would not have returned home.

After my trip to the other planets was over, I was taken to a Saucer Club in Chicago (not on a saucer though). However, I was not allowed to use my own name or tell my story to the group. Neither were they allowed to take my picture and many of them had flash cameras. After that meeting was over, the space men met me and told me that I had not done as I agreed; I had not told my story myself. Bucky, however, knew the wicked ways of this world and he told me that he would help me to have another chance.

I don't know how he did it, but anyway, I was taken to Detroit by the saucer club there and I told of my experience myself and in my own way. This I will always be thankful for. I gave my talk at the Veterans Memorial Building on July 26th, 1955.

Unknown to anyone, a representative of the planet Venus was in the crowd that night and after the meeting, he told me that I had done alright and that I would be allowed to go on another trip into space. No date was set for it though. Many will, no doubt, remember me speaking about that when I talked from the same place on July 28th, two days later.

While in Chicago, scientists and astronomers questioned me. I answered their questions and I also told them about a bridge on the moon, which went from one crater to another. The space folks had built it so they could use their cars which skim along 3 to 5 feet off the ground, and not have to use their space ships.

These same men (scientists) came down to my place later, and said that after observing the moon again, they thought that this thing could be a bridge. They asked me questions for a long time and some times they would nod to one another and say,"He has been there".They wouldn't tell me what I had answered that helped them to draw that conclusion.

One astronomer drove from the west coast, and asked me what it looked like in outer space. I told him that it was inky black. He thanked me, bid me goodbye and left.

Among the many people who have visited me were some men from the Armed Forces. They have measured the place where the saucer came down, and measured the angle of the bit of fence which appears in the picture I took of the saucer. Then they paid me $5, to move one of the posts of the fence and tell no one which way I moved it. In fact one serviceman was at my place so often and felt so much at home, that he walked in the front door and hollered, "Dad, is supper ready"? (He took me out to eat, tho.)

I develop many of my own film rolls and make prints when I take pictures, but I was afraid to develop the roll when I snapped the saucers, since I am very much of an amateur at it. As I said before, I had never heard of saucers, not the flying variety at least, but I knew these things were something most unusual. It was the people who developed the roll who alerted the Armed Forces that I had something which should be investigated.

These men of the Armed Forces bought the clothes which I wore on the saucer. The metal was magnetized even to the eyelets of my shoes. I don't know what type of metal was in the buckles of my over alls, nor do I know whether all the types were magnetized or not. I guess that's why it was wanted, that is, to test it for all such things.

Among the many people who have been down here at Mountain View, was Mrs. Fanny Lowery and her sister, Florence Collins. At that time, Mrs Lowery wanted to know if the space men were coming back. I told her that Bob Solomon had bid me goodbye, but

Bucky said he would try to get back sometimes around the holidays. When Mrs. Lowery was sending out Christmas cards, she sent one addressed to Bucky in care of my ranch. I set the envelope unopened upon the shelf in the hope that Bucky would come. Well, he did come. He arrived at about 1;30 A.M. on December 25th, 1955. He left just about midnight the 25th, so he spent about 22½ hours with me.

Bucky laughed like an eight year old kid when he saw the picture on his card. It was just an advertisement, but it had the picture of 8 or 9 monkeys doing all sorts of wrong things to a new yellow car. They were putting gas in the radiator, antifreeze in the gas tank, and painting it red with a scrub brush. Beneath the picture, it said, "Dont let Anyone Monkey Around Your Car." Written on the back between the lines of advertising was the question, "Does anyone monkey around Saucers like this"?

Bucky said that it was the first gift which had ever been knowingly sent by mail to a person from another planet from a person on earth. He took it back to Venus with him and said he would forever cherish this gift.

While he was visiting me, Bucky left a message for all the world, which I recorded on tape. He also answered Mrs. Lowery's question. Here are his words, exactly as he spoke them...

(This is a tape recording made in the home of Buck Nelson on Christmas day, 1955. My distant cousin, "Bucky", is here with me. Bucky will say a few words to all of you in America and all the world. The next voice you hear will be that of "Bucky" from the planet Venus. O.K. Bucky ....)

- 23 -

BUCKY'S CHRISTMAS MESSAGE TO THE WORLD

I wish to tell all a Merry Christmas, and especially thank Fanny Lowery for her card. Also give her the answer to her question.---Yes, it has happened to our ships, torn apart for souvenirs.

I appreciate such gifts and I know that the giver does not expect anything in return, as we cannot exchange gifts with this Earth. Many know the reason. Buck here can tell all that ask.

Will tell you why I am here. I have just returned from California, then on to see my folks in Colorado. Now here to see you, Buck, and tell the world on this tape recording that this world must give up ATOMIC WEAPONS and WARFARE. The next war, if fought, will be on American soil. America will be destroyed, then civilization all over the world will be destroyed. We are here to see which way this world will use Atomic power, for peace or war. We have stood by and seen other planets, one other, destroy itself. Is this world next? We wonder, and watch and wait.

Again I say, give up your Atomic weapons and may Peace be on this Earth.

I will tell Buck much more that he can tell the world. I know that Buck will want my time here to be spent in a private home-like way, and I also desire it that way, so must say goodbye to all the world...

From

BUCKY of VENUS

I thank you Bucky, for your talk to the people of the world. This is recorded at Buck's Mountain View Ranch, Mountain View, Missouri, Route 1.

End of Tape

(Bucky came to see me December 25, 1955 at about 1:30 AM and left about midnight, December 25, 1955.)

A couple of friends came in to see me on Christmas. They saw Bucky but had no idea that he was anyone special. One of them even tried to sell him some insurance. An insurance policy would do him about as much good as a bicycle wheel on a flying saucer. (Its a shame to call such beautiful heavenly craft by such a name). Insurance, like so many other things we have, would be useless and undesirable on another planet.

We have many things, Bucky said, which are just exactly backward to what they should be. Our advertising often tries to make out that one product is so much better than another when actually it may only be different in some way or another. Advertising, just as anything else should be truthful. Labels on cans, for instance, should tell the contents first, brand names afterward. Take a can of pork and beans; it should be labeled beans and then pork. Why should a sliver of pork have first place over a whole can of beans?

We could eliminate useless duplication in government if our country was divided into, only 3 or 4 parts instead of 48.

Real Estate? My readers can figure that one out, that is, what the space people think about our real rstate.

While I was on the space ship, I saw emblems of the Pyramids on their towels. I asked why they used something of ours like that. They told me that they had seen our civilization go down many times. Then on Christmas, Bucky gave me more information on this. He said that some of the people who built the Pyramids were taken to Mars and Venus and later died on those planets. The stones of the Pyramids were lifted by magnetic power, the same as that used on their space ships. There is a shaft in one of the Pyramids (or was in times past), through which one particular star could be seen. When this star was seen, the Nile would overflow it's banks in three days.

- 25 -

OUR BIBLICAL FLOOD

Atlantis was a Godly nation, largest of the known continents on Earth. They became wise, strong and learned. But, forgetting God, they wanted more power to provide more leisure time pleasure. They had not yet been a war-like nation. They had learned of a power even greater than our Atomic power. They had great, long, large tunnels under their largest city. These were used for research work and experimentation with this new power they were developing. In these new experiments, this new power was let loose and Atlantis was destroyed. It was sunk in the ocean. This was our Biblical Flood. All known lands at that time were flooded, as tidal waves were caused. North America raised up out of the ocean.

Venus has a record of Atlantis going down. It is said, that perhaps some were washed ashore to the new North America. They would degenerate because of living in caves, eating fish and seaweed. Perhaps these people were our first civilization after the flood. Then these people vanished from the Earth, leaving behind many cliff dwellings and evidence of a former civilization. Bucky tells me that the people of Venus and Mars have seen this Earth populated many times only to dissapear. It was populated the last time by many planets who sent their undesirable people here to work out and solve their own problems.

-*- -*- -*-

On June 21st, 1956, I was listening to the radio in my room at the Dressel Home in Washington D.C. (1430 "N" St, NW). Suddenly the program broke as if a news flash was coming in. Instead, it was my cousin, Bucky from Venus. He told me that there was quite a gathering of people in my yard at home in Mountain View, and also that there was plenty of feed in the barrels for my horse and colt and they were well cared for.

These barrels, which hold corn and ground feed, are set in an enclosed porch at the back of the house and are under a good tight roof. John H. Tyrinell had always given my pets good care, so I hadn't really worried about them, but I naturally thought about them a lot, as they are the only family I have. Others have cared for them also. I knew that my friends, the Sherman Lowery's from Clarkston Michigan were at my home but I had no idea that any one else was there until Bucky told me on the radio. This was confirmed when I arrived at the Lowery's on July 2nd, 1956.

The month of March, 1956, I spent in Baltimore and Washington D.C. This was my first visit east on this project. The month of June, 1956 was my second. My job was to tell about the trip I made to Mars, the Moon and Venus, as I had promised the space men I would do.

I am not the first person to be taken to another planet, but I believe I am the first one in recent time to tell about it. (But then, fools will go where angels fear to tread). Some government officials have admitted to me that some of them have been taken to other planets but cannot reveal their identities. All, except one, were disapointed that I couldnt give them more information, but with no scientific training of any kind, I can tell only what I see and am told.

So many people from all walks of life on Earth, have helped me to get this information out, that it is impossible to give them all credit in a booklet of this size. The names used are given because there is a direct connection with the story, one way or another.

Among the many places where I have told my story of my trip have been a number of churches.

Radio and T.V. have had me as a guest on their programs. I always wear bib overalls no matter where I am. They are what I am used to, and I see no reason to change now. The space men tell me it is best that way, also, because people can recognize me easier that way. I think it is something which will fit in with their future plans with me.

Some 1500 people from Mars and Venus are in our nation today. Their help can easily be secured in solving our problems. The files of our Air Force should be opened to the people, that they may know the truth. If people knew the truth, it could help to avert a nuclear war, which would destroy our civilization.

When I was a guest in the home of the Rodney Burgess family in Grand Rapids, Michigan in July, 1956, they also had as their guest, Lee Childers of Detroit. Laura Burgess very thoughtfully put us to sleep in the same room, so we had plenty of time to talk. In fact, we did very little sleeping. Many of the things which the space folks had told Lee were practically the same as had been told to me.

Lee Childers was taken up into a large space ship. His word has been doubted, the same as mine has, but I will vouch for him anytime. He knew the pass words, if you want to call them that.

One thing I did to get ready for my trip was to secure some small American flags. I left one on each planet I visited. On each flag I attached a little label with the words...

"Flag Of The U.S.A. from Planet EARTH
Given to VENUS by BUCK NELSON"

In the years to come, if anyone from our Earth reaches these planets, they will find the U.S. flag with my name on it.

Mrs. Lowery has been taking this down in longhand, between making drapes, receiving my many visitors, opening cans and making coffee. But this tale is getting longer than the tail on the fireball I photographed in January, 1956, so I HAD
BETTER QUIT.

A POSTSCRIPT
By
Fanny Lowery

Being a woman, this looks as if I am trying to get in that proverbial last word.

Anyway, I cant help but think that many people will be interested in some of the bits of proof of Buck's experience. Especially interesting is the trouble to which someone is going to keep these related conditions from being put into print.

After our good friend had returned to Missouri, he wrote to us about the trip. Here is a condensed version of what happened...

"Dear Friends,

I havent been able to find that jar of liquid, marked 'BO BATH', anywhere.

I had a good trip home except that I was taken off the bus at rest stops; once at Toledo and once again at Fort Wayne, Indiana. I was told what not to tell, told not to tell things which prove my story.

Then after I got home, THREE MEN IN BLACK came to my house. They told me to forget all I know about the space ships and where they come from. I showed them my rifle and told them not to come any closer unless they wanted trouble. I am sure the law lets me protect myself from such people. They talked between themselves and said,'Well, you can tell or print your story, because it is so well known anyway, but NEVER TRY TO PROVE IT.

So much of what the Three Men in Black said to me, would be hard to tell, let alone write. So much of it didn't make sense. Anyway I dont scare easy. I dont think I'll be bothered again and I dont think they will bother you for helping me with this work. You can write this for print if you feel that you dare.

I cooperate with government agencies when they come to see me. I do so in all ways, when they let me know who they are. I'm glad I'm an American and I do my best to cooperate. I don't know who these men were".

'Your Friend, Buck '

— *** ——

Related bits of proof are scattered all through Buck's story and a few more are given here.

Some of the proofs depend on timing and conditions. Buck has not had money to buy Saucer books, if he even knew they existed. It is doubtful if he would have been interested in them before the time of the experience which he had. Life was too hard and he was too sick and crippled up to wonder much about folks or other worlds.

In the month of December, 1955, I was informed that Mr. Nelson was a fake and that a very prominent investigator had been down to see Buck, when Buck was not expecting anyone. He reportedly found Buck with all sorts of Flying Saucer books and the Popular Mechanics magazine. He was supposed to have made up his story from these books and magazines.

Well, I couldn't swallow that, because I knew exactly when those books were sent to Buck and where they came from. My sister, Florence, and I had been to see him on the 4th of October, 1955. "Inside the Space Ships" (by George Adamski) had just been sent to him. At the time of Buck's trip, that book was still in the hands of the publisher. Buck told about the light that casts no shadow, just as Adamski did in that book. I had sent him saucer books by different authors, just as soon as I got home. I never met Buck until the Detroit Flying Saucer Club had him as a guest speaker, and so these experiences were told before he ever heard of Adamski.

My son, Nathan and I visited Buck during the holidays. I looked in Buck's guest book and the

- 30 -

name of the person under suspicion appeared right after the signatures of my sister and me.

Nate and I had not been in Buck's house two hours when he told us about the "Book Machine" on Venus. The only place that I had ever found a detailed description of this machine in any book, was in the book which was supposed to have been written psychically (A Dweller on Two Planets), by Phylos Even the size of the machines tallied. I believed Buck before, but when he told me about that machine, that was the clincher as far as I was concerned. At that time the book was extremely hard to get. The Old Prof's Book Shop in Pontiac, Michigan had to send to California to get it.

Bucky's answer on the taped Christmas Message, to my question about people monkeying with their saucers, was that their ships had been torn apart for souvenirs. At that time, none of us had read but a very vague reference to such a thing happening. Then in June, the Roy Tedrick's of Westplains Missouri, loaned us Frank Skully's "Behind the Flying Saucers". This book tells, in a good bit of detail, about earthlings tearing apart saucers for souvenirs.

Photo

Of

Fire

Ball.

- 31 -

A couple of days after we got to Buck's place, the three of us went down the side of the mountain, where Buck knew that larger space ships had landed. There wasn't any marks of their tripod landing gear. We were looking for signs in the earth but instead, we found a sign in the heavens. It was a great CLOUD CROSS in the sky. It must have been anywhere from 3 to 5 miles across it. There wasn't another cloud in that part of the sky.

Buck snapped a picture of a cross in the sky, just a day or two later. Then on January 1st, 1956, Buck got a fire ball on film. (The picture appears on the preceding page).

There is not record of the time when "Big Bo's" picture was taken, but Buck tells us that Bucky brought Bo with him several times. Bucky also took pictures of Teddy which he carried back to Venus. Government agents, when working with Buck, were able to establish Bo's approximate size by the trees in the background and knowing where the camera had set. A brief report of the analysis of Bo's hair was sent to me by Rose Hackett from Baltimore. One of their club members had it analyzed.

When Sherman and I went down to Buck's in June, 1956, we met some of his neighbors; amongst them, Carl Crank and his mother. Carl is the mailman who carried the first piece of mail known to have been sent to another planet. The "Powers that Be" couldn't have picked a nicer guy.

Mrs. Crank, a lady if I ever saw one, was the most gracious hostess one could ever meet. She welcomed us as friends of Buck, and verified that Buck was sick and crippled before the space ships visit. She also named two men in the town who had seen the saucers all day on the day that they first appeared over Buck's place.

Mr. James Hill of Seymour, Missouri, told us that he had been sent by the government to investigate Buck. He found on medical records, that Buck's statement about his health was true. Both James and Mrs. Hill saw space ships at the time they were over Buck's place.

We met quite a number of Buck's friends and found them fine people. They seemed to have plenty of respect for Buck and vouched for his honesty.

An old saying goes, "A prophet is not without honor, save in his own country and in his own house." (Matt.XIII.57). Well, Buck seems to be an exception. Mr. and Mrs. Cristan, who live only five or six miles across country from Buck, had him tell about his trip at the local Sunday School.

Although severely criticized for it, they did not back down on the issue. They had never read any saucer books, either.

THAT TAKES MORE THAN COURAGE..
THAT TAKES REAL FAITH
The End.

1958

" FLYING SAUCER CONVENTION "
There will be a Saucer Convention at
" BUCK'S MOUNTAIN VIEW RANCH "
the last Saturday and Sunday of June
1958
EVERY ONE WELCOME
All come..... Young and Old.

Lecturers wanted to speak on platform. All sightings wanted. Come and tell it yourself. Musical acts wanted, and any other acts that are suitable for a Saucer Convention. Write to;

BUCK'S MOUNTAIN VIEW RANCH
Buck Nelson   Rte. 1
MOUNTAIN VIEW, MISSOURI

ANNOUNCING - - -   BUCK'S FLYING SAUCER CLUB

At many of my lectures, it has often been brought up that a club should be formed for those interested in exchanging U.F.O. information, pictures, clippings etc. This service is FREE to all interested. As mail will be heavy at the home office, please send postage (when writing Buck Nelson) if reply is desired. No other charges... Names and addresses will be printed, so members may write each other direct. Send your name and address to;

Buck's Mountain View Ranch
Route 1
Mountain View, Missouri.

Readers of my book are invited to camp out on my property, FREE. No charge for space. Free wood for your fireplace. Free water. Bring your own tent, house car or camping outfit.
Camping out is free any time of the year and during the...
CONVENTION.
BUCK NELSON.

MEMBERS OF BUCK'S FLYING SAUCER CLUB

Gertrude W. Tyler
Herman Tyler

Mr. and Mrs. Roy Tedrick

Kesiah

Mrs. David Ackerman

Edmund Kiernan

Mrs. Fanny C. Lowery

Louis C. Chaiet

Mr. and Mrs. M.J. Shanander

Frank T. Bailey, Jr.

Mr. James L. Hill

Miss Dorothy Orrison

Dr. Adolph G. Dittmar

Miss Ruby Polley

Harvey L. Duggan

E.M. Hill

Mary Jane Ashman

BOOKS and PERIODICALS

CENTER OF THE WORLD

Address; 1226 H. St. N.W. Washington 5, D.C.
Desires speakers in advanced Religion, Health, Saucers and other fields related to the New Age. Write for details and reservations. "We gather the world for advanced thought". Dept. B-K--4.

FLYING SAUCERS CHART

A complete visual survey of the U.F.O. phenomena. Picturing shapes, maneuvers, formations, speeds, sizes, colors etc... Also sketches of space people... Over 1370 items...
Price. $1.00

Order from;
Keziah, [redacted]

ABOARD A FLYING SAUCER
by Truman Betherum

Here is a book of adventure that you could hardly help being incredulous. Send your order direct to: Truman Betherum. [redacted] Send $3.20 for an autographed copy. Price includes tax and postage. Mr. Betherum is also accepting orders for his new book- <u>Facing Reality</u>. This will soon be available.

UFOrum --

Publication of the Grand Rapids Flying Saucer Club.. Issued monthly..Subscriptions; FREE WILL Offering. Write; UFOrum, Box 142-Rte,1. Ada Mich..

LITTLE LISTENING POST

Published at; 4811 Illinois, N.W. Washington D.C. 6 issues for $2.00.

U F O SPEAKERS - - -

Any Saucer Club (or UFO Organization) wanting a speaker, would do well to write;
Mr. Lee Childers Jr.

Mr. Childers has been up into space now for the fourth time and can tell your club about it. Write to him for information.

U.F.O. RESEARCH

We will welcome you to take part in our research. Your photographs, clippings, UFO sightings etc, will be welcome. Send them in with permission to publish them. None can be returned. Send them to; Buck's Mountain View Ranch, Mountain View, Mo.

BUCK NELSON, writer of this booklet, is available for lecture and will go on lecture tours. Write for dates or other information.

SAUCER DETECTOR

Hang from ceiling of House.

If a magnetized bar is hung on a string, about 18 inches long, it will act as a "Saucer Detector". It must be hung in a place free from any draft. If there is a Space Craft over the house, the magnetized bar will be drawn upward. If the Space Craft circles the house, the bar will move in a circle. This magnetized bar can be purchased at most radio repair shops. The magnetized bar can be as small as one inch in length.

April 11, 1958

REC- 23   43-1357-424

Reverend Bill Britton

EX-135

Dear Mr. Britton:

Your letter dated March 13, 1958, has been brought to my attention.

In answer to your inquiry, I wish to advise that the FBI has not conducted any investigation such as you described since such matters do not come within the scope of this Bureau's authority. I am taking the liberty, however, of referring a copy of your letter to the Director of Special Investigations, The Inspector General, Department of the Air Force, Building Tempo E, Fourth and Adams Drive, Southwest, Washington, D. C.

Sincerely yours,

J. Edgar Hoover

John Edgar Hoover
Director

MAILED 5
APR 11 1958
COMM-FBI

1 - Kansas City (65-1544)
rebulet 3-21-58 to Britton and urlet 4-2-58

Copy of incoming from Britton dated 3-13-58 to O.S.I. by form.

NOTE: Bufile 43-13592-413 is a letter dated 3-13-58 from Britton inquiring as to whether the FBI had interrogated one Buck Nelson of Mountain View, Missouri, regarding his extravagant claims concerning flying saucers. Britton alleged that Nelson was forbade to speak of his activities by FBI. Bulet 3-21-58 to Britton was an in-absence reply requesting Kansas City to contact Nelson in this regard.

Publications forwarded by Kansas City currently make no reference to the FBI.

DCL:hjf
(4)

Tolson
Boardman
Belmont
Mohr
Nease
Parsons
Rosen
Tamm
Trotter
Clayton
Tele. Room
Holloman
Gandy

64 APR 17 1958

www.ingramcontent.com/pod-product-compliance
Lightning Source LLC
Chambersburg PA
CBHW081136170426
43197CB00017B/2881